MARGARET MORGAN
and
MARY MORGAN PEDLOW

Memorial

GLAZED PEACH

SNOW POPPY

Typeset in Akzidenz Grotesk, mostly

Art created with scissors, paper, crayons,
a digital camera, Illustrator, and Photoshop

Book design by Laurie Rosenwald

Illustrations by Laurie Rosenwald

Published by Bloomsbury U.S.A. Children's Books
175 Fifth Avenue, New York, New York 10010
Distributed to the trade by Macmillan

Library of Congress
Cataloging-in-Publication Data
Rosenwald, Laurie.
All the wrong people have self-esteem :
an inappropriate book for young ladies
(or, frankly, anybody else) / by Laurie
Rosenwald. — 1st U.S. ed.
p.   cm.
ISBN-13: 978-1-59990-240-1
ISBN-10: 1-59990-240-0
1. Teenage girls—Life skills guides.
2. Teenage girls—Conduct of life.
I. Title.
HQ798.R66 2008
305.235'20207—dc22
2008014386

First U.S. Edition 2008
Printed in China
10 9 8 7 6 5 4 3 2 1

All papers used
by Bloomsbury U.S.A. are
natural, recyclable products
made from wood grown
in well-managed forests. The
manufacturing processes
conform to the environmental
regulations of the
country of origin.

this book
is dedicated to my

DADDY

robert rosenwald
1920–2006

are you
ready?

all the wrong people have self-esteem

laurie rosenwald

bloomsbury

UP TO AND
INCLUDING
BUT NOT LIMITED TO

why libras make great zookeepers and submarine operators

where babies *really* come from

kicked out of yoga class

your breasts:
what do they **mean?**

what's with the rubber bracelets?

the PMS collection agency

is the earth really *worth* saving?

really extreme makeover:
25,185 days to a better **you!**

you smell lonely

what is this book, ANYWAY?

if you've ever felt
that you don't deserve
bottled water, this book is for you.
if you're a vegetarian but you eat meat,
this book is for you.

if you've ever stolen a lipstick, this book is for you.

on the other hand
if you haven't or you don't, and everything's
perfect, you should read it anyway,

because nobody likes a winner.

why *do* all the wrong people have self-esteem?

interesting people are full of doubt. people who are *totally* sure their way is the only way are *always wrong*. i think self-esteem is a myth perpetrated by psychologists, movie stars, magazines, and the pharmaceutical industry. they want you to think something's wrong with you because you don't have self-esteem like you "should." oh, please!
georgia o'keeffe, beethoven, and mark twain all had their doubts, but managed somehow to get a few things done. and so can you.

sometimes i feel like i don't deserve bottled water.

besides, tap is the new bottled.

"REASONS TO BE CHEERFUL, PART 3"

IS A SONG BY IAN DURY AND THE BLOCKHEADS. IN 1979 IT REACHED NUMBER 3 IN THE UK CHARTS. IN IT HE LISTS MANY, INCLUDING:

GENEROSITY AND POLITENESS, PORRIDGE, YELLOW SOCKS, EQUAL VOTING RIGHTS FOR MEN AND WOMEN, CARROT JUICE, JAMAICAN TROMBONIST RICO RODRIGUEZ BEING RELEASED FROM PRISON, AND A CURE FOR SMALLPOX.

FOR ME, A FEW WOULD BE ORANGEY-RED, FINGERPAINT GREEN, NEW YORK CITY, MY FRIENDS, PETS, DAIRY PRODUCTS, BULGOGI, LIPSTICK, MUSIC, DANCING, CRUSHES, SNEAKERS, CARAN D'ACHE CRAYONS, GLUE, GUYS, AL GREEN, OIL PAINT, EUROPE, BRENDA, PARTIES, AND SHARPIES.

WHAT ARE YOURS?

1

2

3

4

5

6

7

8

9

D.I.Y.

ADVICE FOR YOUNG LADIES

BECAUSE YOU ALREADY KNOW!

Hello, young ladies! You are almost _____ by now, so full of hope, so full of dreams, so full of _____. If you want to live a long and happy life, here are s rules to live by. First and most important, wait as long as possible before you have _____. This can lead to an unwanted _____, and you have enough on plate already. Right, girls? Don't let any of those _____ from school pressure you into _____. They might try to flatter you and tell you that you are so _____ Don't you believe it! Look, it's not the guys who risk _____, or even worse: _____. If you and your boyfriend are really ready for _____, make sure are protected. Seek help from a qualified _____ or maybe even ask your parents. _____, _____, and rock 'n' roll? Forget it. _____ are danger _____ and driving don't mix. Many teens are killed on the _____ each and you don't want to be one of them. _____ can be a problem. Yes, even if you just stick to an occasional _____. You don't want to become an alcoholic! Don't _____. If you do, quit immediately. Eat plenty of fresh _____ and _____. Remember, it's not good to be too _____ or too _____. Anorexia and obesity are major problems facing teens, but there are many organizations out there to help. On the other hand, if you're 6'7", you're too tall. Nothing to do about that one! If you're depressed, there are many things that help.

_____, _____, _____, and, yes, sometimes _____. The main thing with depression is that you ask people that you trust to help you. Don't keep it to yourself. Remember, it's nothing that twenty-five years of intensive, expensive _____ couldn't cure!

THE SHOCKING TRUTH:

WHERE BABIES really COME FROM

ABSTINENCE, ONLY...

Advocates for **"Abstinence-Only"** education believe that schools should only teach about abstinence from sex, and should not provide information on how to obtain and use condoms and other contraception. In light of conservative support of an "Abstinence-Only" S-E- E-D-U- - -T-I- -N policy in our public schools, we thought it was the very least we could do to present a fairly informative, kind of accurate, but not nearly comprehensive account of, well, you know. If teens learn just a few of the ghastly, disgusting "facts," they'll be less likely to try to find out all of them through the Internet and stuff. Or even worse, experience. We offer the following report: The sexual act is best demonstrated by putting your finger into an electrical outlet. First you must wet your finger. See? Sex may cause an "organism." An organism might pop out and make you scream something like, "Would you like fries with that?" Then the organism turns into a tadpole. If you are wearing rubber, don't worry, because you are grounded, and protected from the organism. Before the sexual act, put on new sneakers and brush your tongue. Put on your Usher CD, and try some French Twisting. Warning: You may experience one or more side effects, such as diaper rash, global thermonuclear meltdown, or tummy ache.

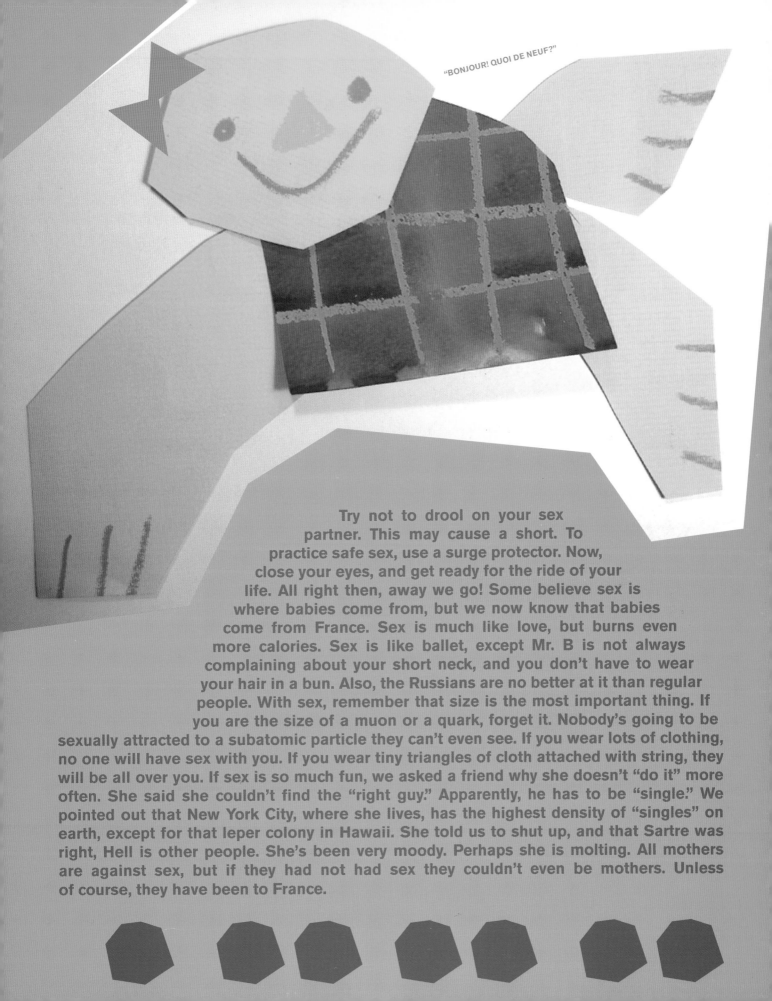

Try not to drool on your sex partner. This may cause a short. To practice safe sex, use a surge protector. Now, close your eyes, and get ready for the ride of your life. All right then, away we go! Some believe sex is where babies come from, but we now know that babies come from France. Sex is much like love, but burns even more calories. Sex is like ballet, except Mr. B is not always complaining about your short neck, and you don't have to wear your hair in a bun. Also, the Russians are no better at it than regular people. With sex, remember that size is the most important thing. If you are the size of a muon or a quark, forget it. Nobody's going to be sexually attracted to a subatomic particle they can't even see. If you wear lots of clothing, no one will have sex with you. If you wear tiny triangles of cloth attached with string, they will be all over you. If sex is so much fun, we asked a friend why she doesn't "do it" more often. She said she couldn't find the "right guy." Apparently, he has to be "single." We pointed out that New York City, where she lives, has the highest density of "singles" on earth, except for that leper colony in Hawaii. She told us to shut up, and that Sartre was right, Hell is other people. She's been very moody. Perhaps she is molting. All mothers are against sex, but if they had not had sex they couldn't even be mothers. Unless of course, they have been to France.

Q:

WHY DO GIRLS FIGHT WITH THEIR MOTHERS?

A:

I thought this was a no-brainer until I asked my friend's mother, Dorothée, who is French and actually has a brain. She said (and I quote), "Laureee, you are so stupeed! C'est evident! Uv courze zey fight! Zees eez naturellement becauzz when zee daughterz are zee teenahjerz, at exactement zees point zee muzzer eez going sroo zee shange of life, where she eeez loozing 'er own beauté and 'er sexoooualeeeté! And zeee daughterz are just begeeening zere wonderfool sexualeeté! And zey are so beeootyfoool! So zee muzzers are zumetimes jalouze of zer daughterz, zo of courze zey must fight!"

Zee daughterz always win. Mostly.

if i hear about another fabulooney *sex in the city* type book or film about *gossip* or tv show about *lipstick* or *prada* or even *shoes* i'm gonna puke all over my chuck taylors.

chick? maybe.

and what's with the *manolos?*

please,

if fifteen-year-old girls are really wearing fifteen hundred dollar shoes, there is something very, very wrong.

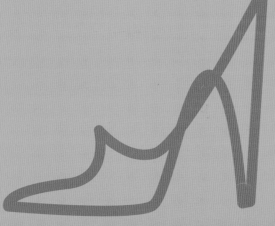

i hate chick lit.

a suggestion:
try some jane austen, baby.

LET'S PLAY

ODD

but not

PECULIAR

AN INCREDIBLY ANNOYING GAME
YOU CAN PLAY ONLY ONCE
IN YOUR LIFE.

**Well, as a
victim, anyway. But you can**

ENRAGE

YOUR FRIENDS

* FOR YEARS TO COME!

*Not the same friends,
of course.

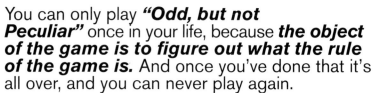

You can only play **"Odd, but not
Peculiar"** once in your life, because **the object
of the game is to figure out what the rule
of the game is.** And once you've done that it's
all over, and you can never play again.

You're always right, because only you know the
rule. You tell them to just start playing with you,
taking turns, and they'll figure it out, eventually.
Here goes:

You say, "Strawberry, but not peach!
And remember, I'm always right!"
They say, "Grape, but not cherry!"
You say, "WRONG!"
Then you say, "Cherry, but not grape!"
They say, "But I just said . . . !"
You say, "Well, you were wrong. But go
ahead . . . try another one."
They say, "Cashew, but not walnut."
You say, "Wrong!"
You say, "Peanut butter, but not jam."
They say, "Jelly, but not jam."
You say, "RIGHT!"
They say, "Really? I was right? Why?"
And you say, "Well when you guess that, you've
won. Madonna, but not Britney. Keep going."
They keep being wrong. And sometimes right,
but they don't know why.
You say, "Silly, but not stupid . . ."

*Here's the rule: The first word in the pair has
a double letter.* Simple!
I had a nervous breakdown trying to figure it out,
especially as I was with a big boatload of idiots
(or so I thought, as usual) who guessed it first.
**The evil trick thing is, the pairs don't have
to RELATE at ALL!** That's what throws you off.
When I was barking mad, I said,

"I GIVE UP!
ISHKABIBBLE, but not PEACH!"

And I was right. By the way, "Jelly, but not peanut
butter" is a WRONG answer, because they
both have double letters.

LIFE

THIS PHILOSOPHY
comes from a Danish proverb:

*Lykken er ikke
det værste vi har,
Og om lidt
er kaffen klar!*

ISN'T THE WORST THAT WE HAVE, AND PRETTY SOON COFFEE IS SERVED!

in other words

As bad as things are, things aren't that bad.

(Actually, if they are, call the police.)

When I was twelve I

Nobody gave me enough presents, and I felt I deserved them. And I loved the thrill, being good at it. Bonwit Teller was a posh department store which stood on the corner of 57th Street and Fifth Avenue. The store doesn't exist anymore, and neither does my bad habit. I don't do that anymore. Also, I don't smoke. I don't drink and drive. I don't eat lard. Too much at stake. Life is good. But that day long ago, I was with my best friend, Little Carol. In the dressing rooms, I put a Sonia Rykiel peasant skirt under my peasant skirt. As we walked out, I noticed a size 22 lady looking through the size four Paco Rabanne minidresses. As we got in the elevator, she quickly moved behind us, putting a wrestler's hold around both our throats, not saying a word. On the main floor everyone got out and she silently pressed the "B" button. In terror, we descended to the basement, where we were searched and questioned separately. I told lies, but Little Carol told the truth to an ex-marine with shoulders a yard apart, a buzz cut, and Old Glory pinned to his lapel. Carol's mother was shocked. My mother was "hurt." Little Carol went on to become a respected physicist, and I became, you know, whatever it is I am today.

got caught shoplifting.

Everybody said I did it for the attention.
Everybody was wrong. I did it for the *stuff.*
Sure, it was a learning experience.
But I didn't learn anything from it.

OR DID I?

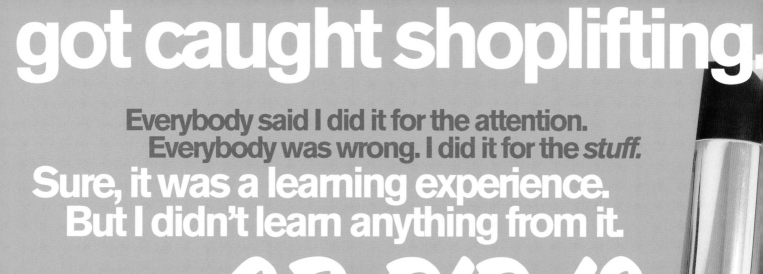

I will still do anything
for free makeup. I'm
obsessed. I worked for a
stupid magazine for years,
for example.
Just for the SWAG! And
packaging is everything.
Shu Uemura. Nars.
And Comme des Garcons
scent. The good stuff. God,
I'm shallow.
My excuse is that using
makeup is
sort of like painting.

THE PMS COLLEC

My pal Dave owed me some money. Kind of a lot of money. After more than a year, he still hadn't paid me back. Aargh! One day I was suffering from advanced PMS. Ranting and raving, completely out of control. Among other things, I was so mad about *this. Mad, I tell you!* I tracked him down. I called him. It was 4 A.M. I shrieked like a banshee: "GIVE ME MY MONEY! MY MONEY! NOW! RIGHT NOW OR I'LL MURDER YOU! AAAAAAAAAAAAAAARRRRRRRRGH!" He was frightened out of his wits, but I felt much better when I hung up the phone. And even better when he came over the next morning with the whole amount. That's when it hit me: Why not start a PMS Collection Agency? A collection agency is a company that hunts people down and threatens them if they don't pay their bills. My agency would be staffed by a rotating staff of hysterical, PMS-ing girls, each at the frightening peak of the emotional roller coaster. Wouldn't that be great? The girls screaming their heads off! Demented! Everybody wins. Let it all out, girls. The crazier the better. "YOU MUST PAY! PAY NOW! OR ELSE! "

IT WILL BE A HUGE SUCCESS!

TION AGENCY

IT'S PAYBACK TIME BABY

GIVE ME MY MONEY!

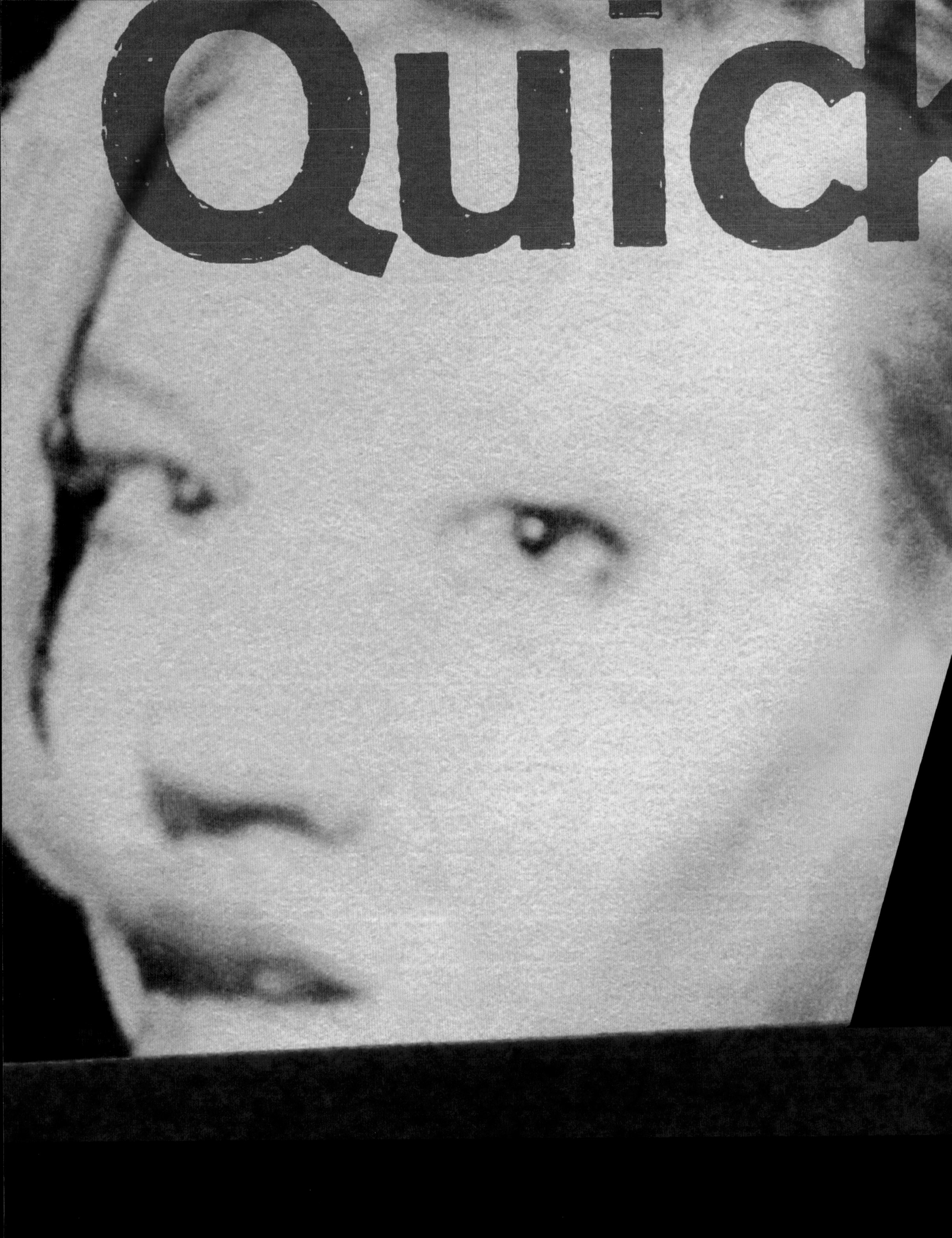
Quick

Comebacks!
All-Purpose!
Handy, Dandy!

THINGS TO SAY WHEN YOU DON'T KNOW WHAT TO SAY:

1 Well, it's nothing that 25 years of intensive psychoanalysis couldn't cure!

2 I'll have to talk to my horse about it.

3 I'm sorry you feel that way.

4 You know the way you are? Well, don't be that way!

AND HERE'S A NEW TREND I HATE SO PLEASE DON'T SAY IT:

You're not a very happy person, are you?

Just come out and say "F--- You!"

What's the POINT in saving the planet if it's full of self-righteous, hypocritical marketing executives?
Yeah! Anyone can slap a leaf logo on a HUMMER and call it "GREEN." Enough!

tired of GREEN?

try PURPLE

the most radical,
subversive thing
you can be is
CHEERFUL
SO

Cheer

crayola magenta

mommy's scarf

the wrong blusher

hippie/prune

goofy grape

wino

send in the choppers

bell bottom

O f course you should keep recycling and wearing vegetarian sneakers and organic cotton underpants and drinking fair trade mochaccinos and using rhubarb & green tea conditioner and cruelty-free lip gloss and driving cars that run on Mazola and buying funny-looking lightbulbs and caring about the polar bears drowning. Of course you should. It's just that I'm tired of all this green marketing. Marketing should involve a shopping cart and milk and bananas!

JOIN THE PURPLE MOVEMENT!

TEN PURPLE THINGS YOU CAN DO:

Thing 1:
I hate lists like this.
Here's what you can do with
your *&%##@*!&#@ list:

Thing 2:
DON'T TELL
PEOPLE
WHAT TO
DO!

UP!

IT MAY NEVER
HAPPEN!

SO KEEP   RECYCLING
AND GET ON WITH IT. NEXT!

By the way, did you know that **TEENAGERS** is an anagram for **EATS GREEN** ?

out

LOL :) :-) Emoticons in general

Apostrophes

The Green Movement

Facebook

Tattoos

S, XS

Prada, Gucci, Juicy, bla bla bla

Cappuccini, caffe latte, café con leche

Macchiati both caffe and latte, espressi

both singolo and doppio, venti anything

Chai Latte and flavored teas

Smoothies

Web sites

Bad boys

Scented candles, Fruity-smelling things

Designer handbags

iPods, iPhones

Pasta

"Hot"

Collecting stuff

Shaved, pierced, or tattooed

Running

Meeting online

Soccer

Dating

Glaring

Scrambled

Jeans of any persuasion***

The WorldWideInterWebNet

***A note about jeans, high vs. low: I have to be honest

LTM* or INLWYILAY**

Commas

The Purple Movement

Facebook

Designer moles and freckles

XM (Extra Medium)

Anything you haven't worn in 6 months

Coffee.

Tea, too.

as in: "I'LL HAVE A SMALL

COFFEE, PLEASE"

Chocolate milk

Night lights

Sad boys

Murphy's Oil Soap

Going out without bag. The Joy of Pockets!

iCE CREAM

Noodles

"Dreamy" "Attractive"

Giving away everything you collect

Baked, Mashed, or Fried

Skipping

Meeting on lunch line

Futbol

Sleepovers

Winking

Sunnyside up

Skirts

Radio

with you, by the time this book comes out, I'll either be right or wrong. And not for long!

in

Nerds

**I'm Not Laughing With You, I'm Laughing At You

*Laughing To Myself

COFFEE
TEA, TOO!

IN: NOODLES!

LATIN

just plain bizarre

things i found on facebook:

Israeli Palestinian conflict muffins

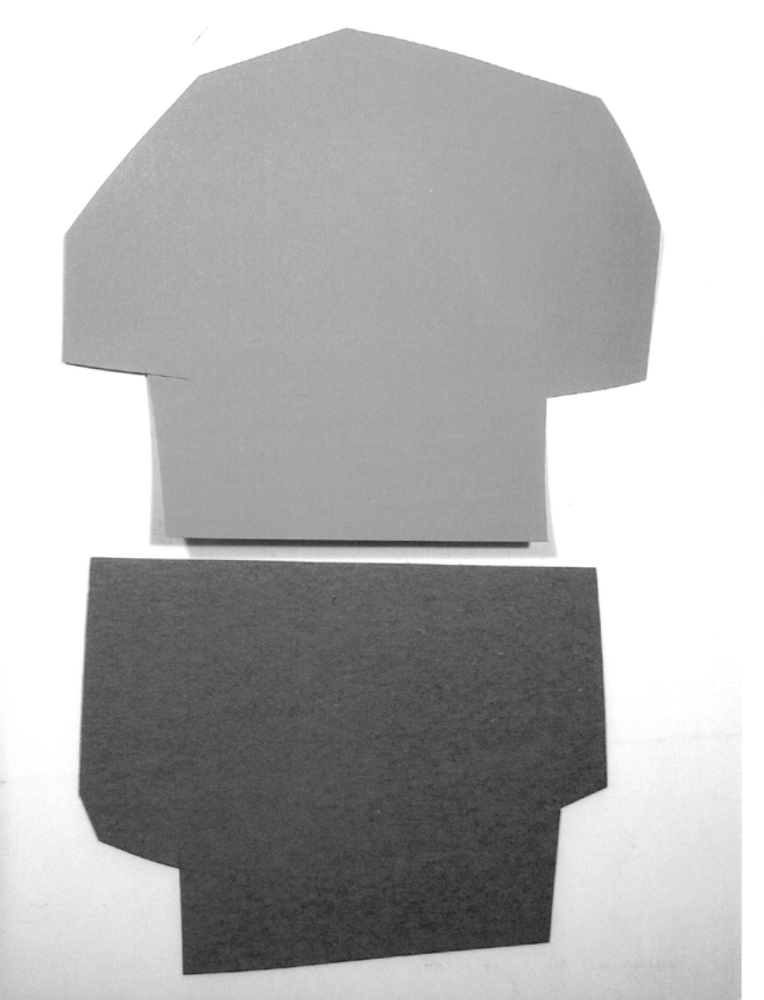

i taught my cats to spoon.
they're from queens so they
picked it up right away.
in fact, they really got into it!
but after a while they wanted
to branch out–
i guess they were bored.
they wanted to do this thing where
we were a butter dish, 2 napkin rings,
and a salad fork.

i said nothing doing.
this is too weird for me.
it's over.

I'D RATHER BE *THAT* KIND OF MODEL ...with a flower!

i wish i looked like a model

I'D RATHER BE *THAT* KIND OF MODEL ...with a swan neck!

it's always some-thing

i want to be alone!

me, too.

I HOPE THINGS ARE BET

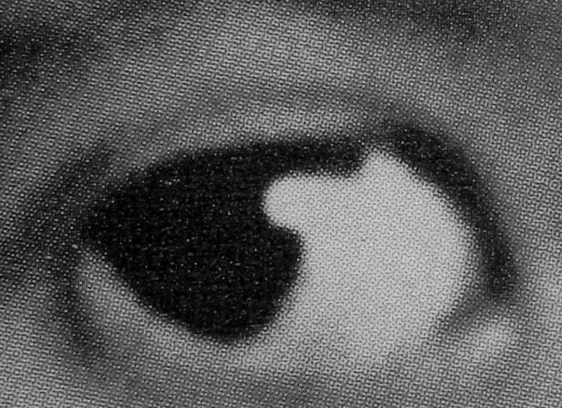

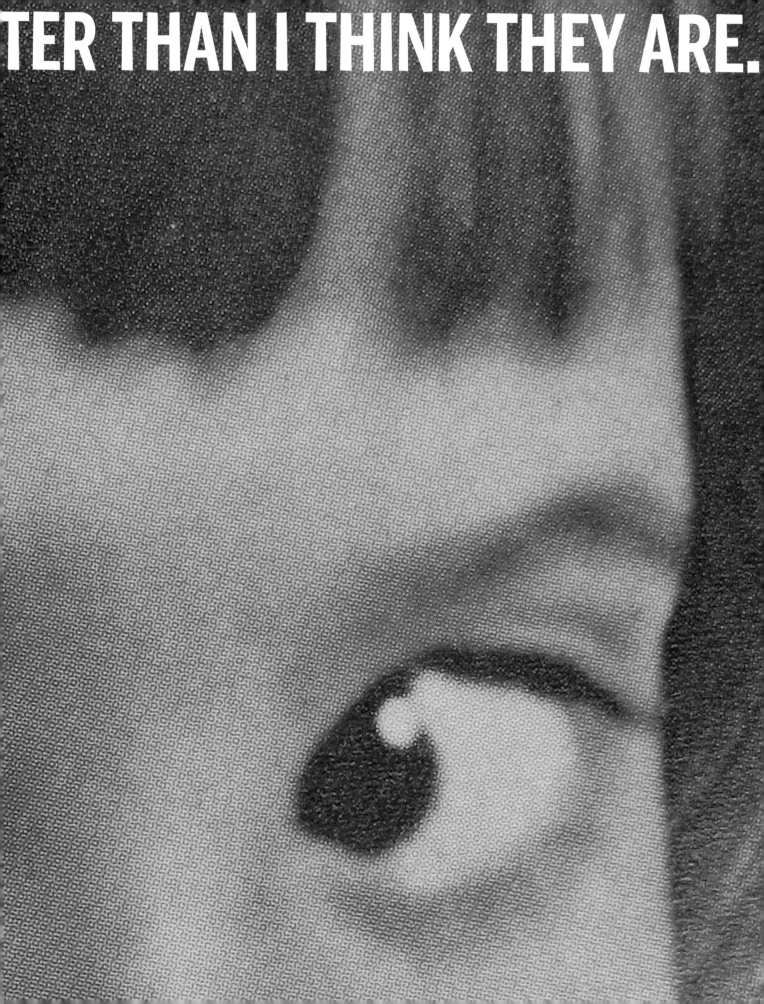

one

problem is that I think I'm smarter than all my friends.

for

example, last
Wednesday I was in
a big rush to get someplace.
I got a ride with some friends.
I'd just washed my hair,
so I stuck my head
out of the window, brushing.
By the time we got there
it was beautifully blow-dried.
I was proud of my multitasking abilities,
so I shared this information with my friend Yetta Tomashoff.

Do you know what she said?
"Do you really think that's a good idea?

That city air out there is so... **dirty!"**

And everybody thinks she's smart! I thought, but did not say, *Where do you think the air in your hair dryer comes from,*

the Swiss Alps?

Can you imagine?

AND ALL THE GIRLS ARE
VERY PRETTY : BUT NOT
AS PRETTY AS YOU!
LOVE
DAD

Albert MONIER
PARIS - Matin d'Automne, Quai d'Anjou
Sujet existant en gravure décorative (format 47 x

addy's

DID YOU EVER CONSIDER THIS?

your natural hair will never be more beautiful than it is now. 40-year-olds are trying to fake what you have.

unless you want purple and green stripes.
that's another story!

Lonely Man

Lonely

Lonely Nig

Lonely Nig

Lonely No

Lonely No

Lonely People

She's About A

Show Me The

Singing For Th

Lonely

Sad So Lon

ry Of A Lon

I've decided to "come out" as a chronically lonely person. I think it's the last taboo. I like to be alone but I don't like to *have* to be. So I'm always looking for people to be with. Apparently, I'm not alone. I googled "Lonely" song lyrics and found several hundred. My favorite one is called "You Smell Lonely."

friends

from many lands
(most of them sweden)

SWEDEN

Look how cute this guy is. Let's call him "Dave." Because his name is Dave. He's a bad boy! Until he started wearing his Peruvian "chullo" hat. It turns him into an instant moron. And yet. Look how cute he is.

dave

(pronounced *dave*)

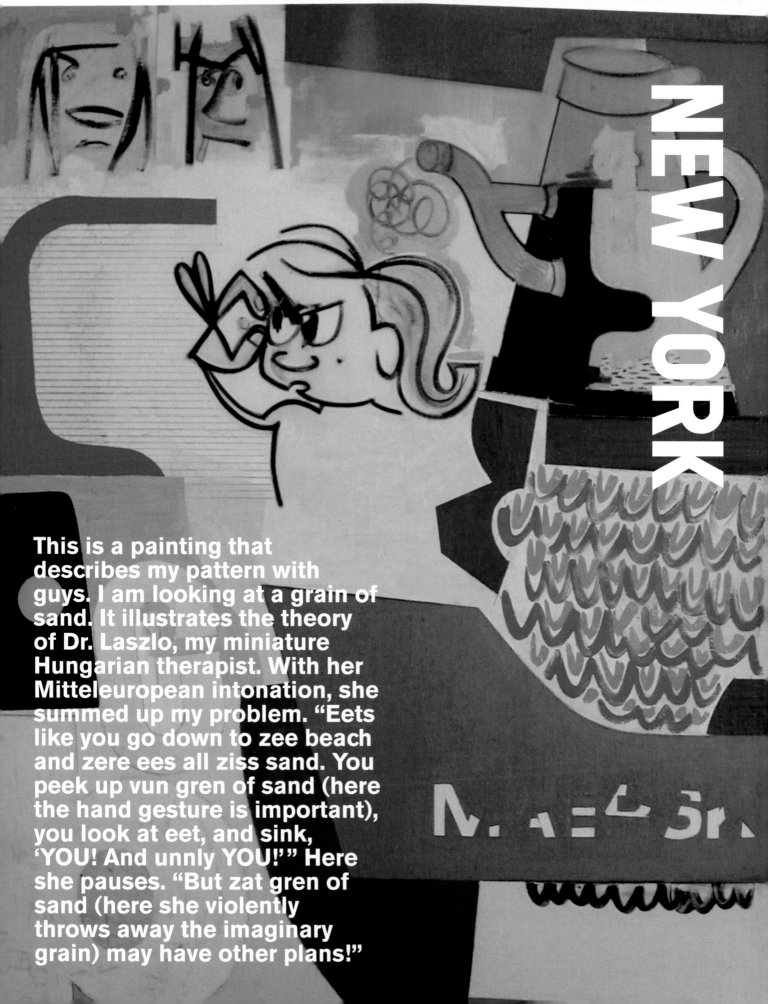

This is a painting that describes my pattern with guys. I am looking at a grain of sand. It illustrates the theory of Dr. Laszlo, my miniature Hungarian therapist. With her Mitteleuropean intonation, she summed up my problem. "Eets like you go down to zee beach and zere ees all ziss sand. You peek up vun gren of sand (here the hand gesture is important), you look at eet, and sink, 'YOU! And unnly YOU!'" Here she pauses. "But zat gren of sand (here she violently throws away the imaginary grain) may have other plans!"

THE MEMBER O

by CARSON McCULLE

It's about a girl named Frankie whose brother Jarvis is getting married to a girl named Janice. And Frankie wants to be part of everything. BUT you know how couples say:

WE WE THINK IT'S SO COOL, OR

WE JUST DON'T LIKE CHEESECAKE, OR

WE QUIT SMOKING, OR WE

OR EVEN LOVED THAT movie

WE CAUGHT A COLD?

F TH WEDDING

RS

(a book i recommend)

She thinks when Janice
  or Jarvis say "We," it includes her.
When she's told that it doesn't,
she says something like, "But Janice and Jarvis are

THE 'WE' OF ME"

They drive off together, leaving her behind.
I always identified with her.
But you know what I feel like now?

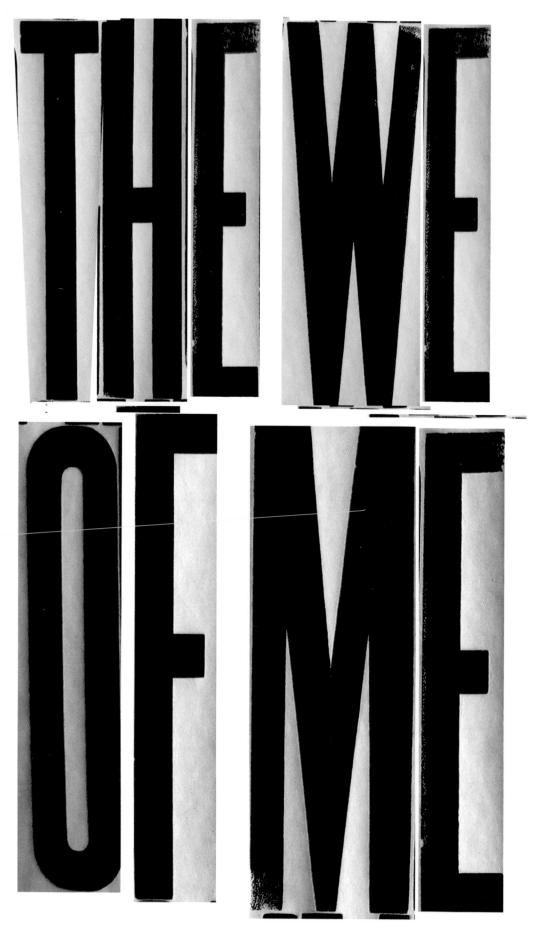

THE WE OF ME

I know it sounds like psychobabble.

i'm a vegetarian

except I eat meat

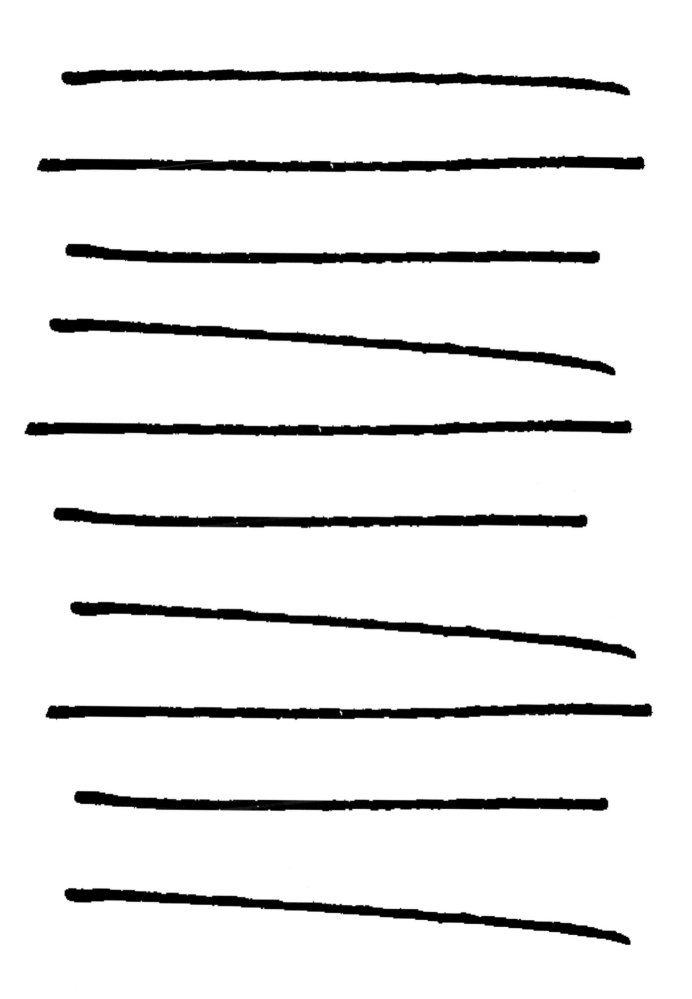

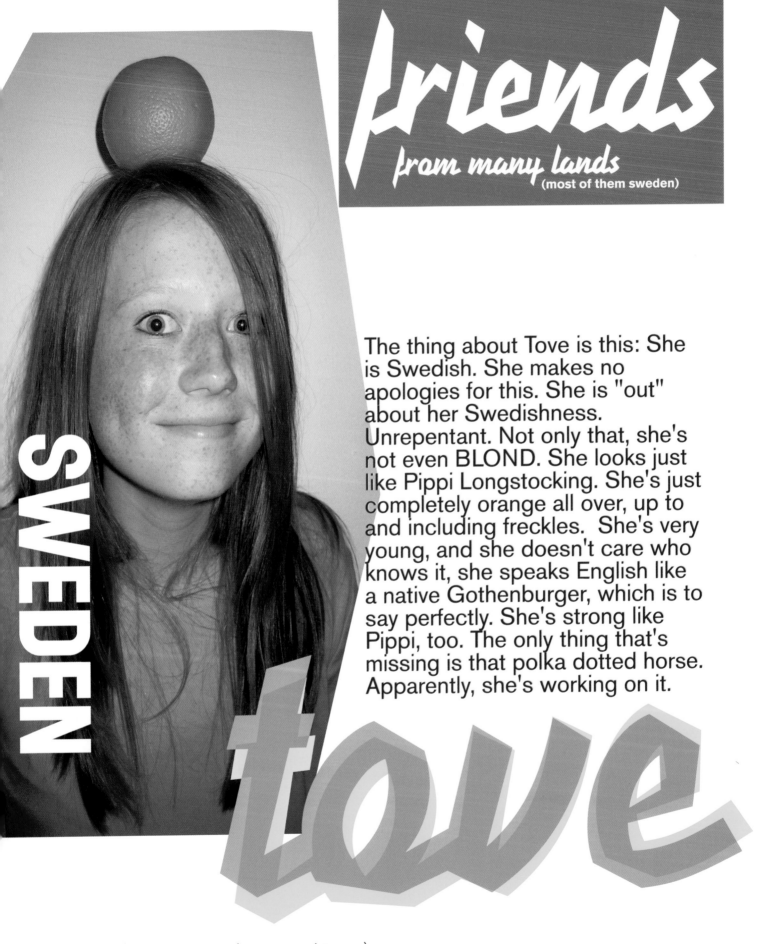

friends
from many lands
(most of them sweden)

SWEDEN

The thing about Tove is this: She is Swedish. She makes no apologies for this. She is "out" about her Swedishness. Unrepentant. Not only that, she's not even BLOND. She looks just like Pippi Longstocking. She's just completely orange all over, up to and including freckles. She's very young, and she doesn't care who knows it, she speaks English like a native Gothenburger, which is to say perfectly. She's strong like Pippi, too. The only thing that's missing is that polka dotted horse. Apparently, she's working on it.

tove

(pronounced *toovay*)

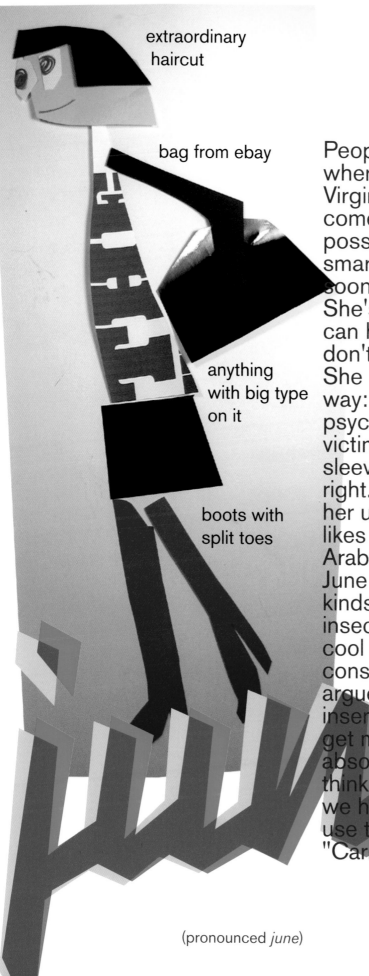

extraordinary
haircut

bag from ebay

anything
with big type
on it

boots with
split toes

june

(pronounced *june*)

VIRGINIA

People are always asking June where she's from. She's from Virginia, but she sounds like she comes from London via Neptune or possibly Alabama. June is super smart. She was ready for MIT as soon as she learned her ABC's. She's going to be a PHD. Anything can hurt her feelings. And please don't say anything about her hair. She describes her bedroom this way: "It's not a bedroom, it's a psychosis." June is a fashion victim, and she was saving up for a sleeve that cost $375.00. That's right. A sleeve. I think she orders her underpants from Paris. She likes to make videos and listens to Arab Strap and the Sneaker Pimps. June eats only salad. Different kinds of salad. Nobody is as insecure as June, and nobody is as cool as June. She's a kind and considerate friend, so we often argue about how I'm a mean, insensitive poopoohead. I always get mad when she won't tell me absolutely everything she is thinking at every moment. Finally we had to invent a signal word we use to stop arguing. The word is "Carnation."

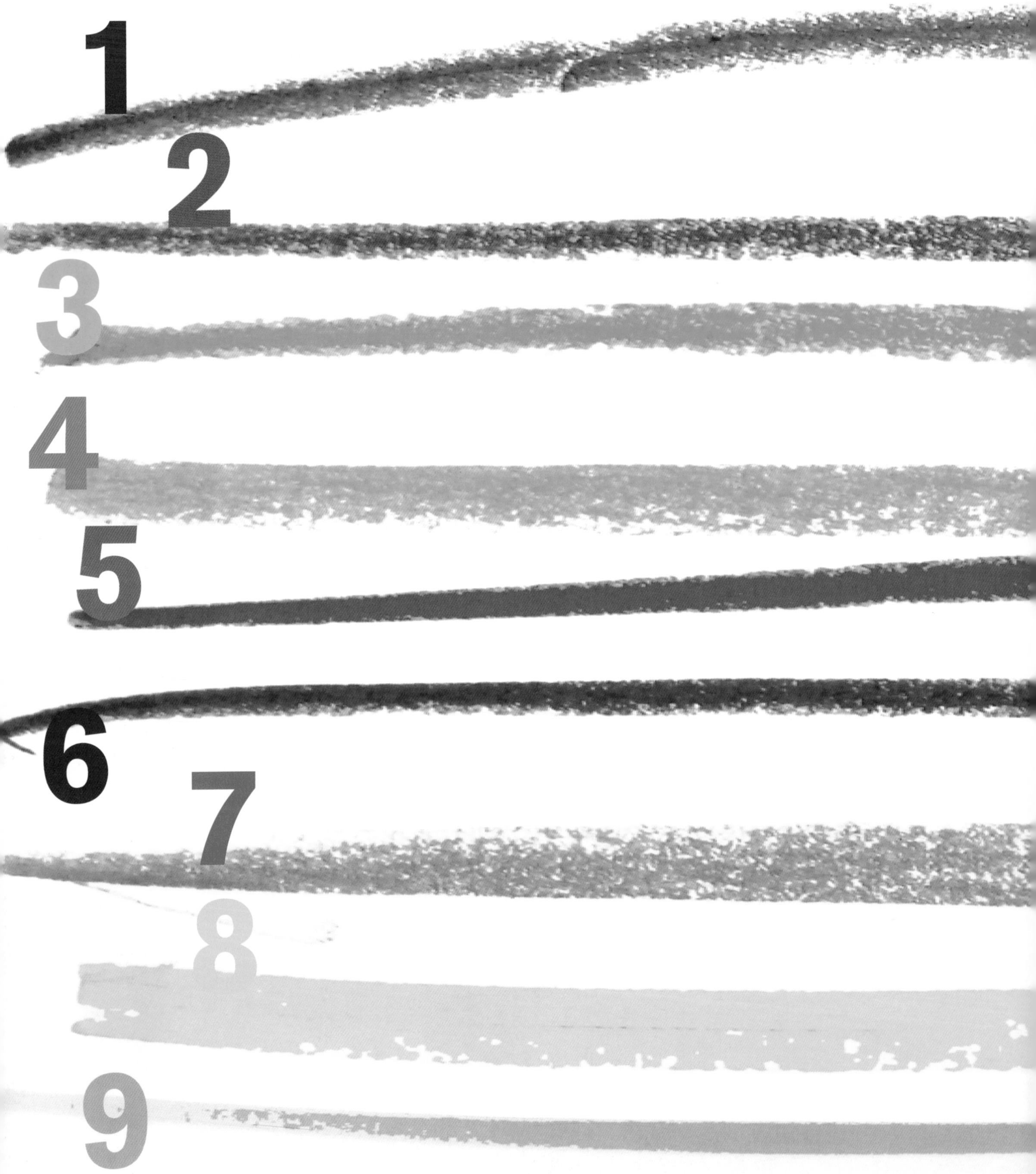

1

2

3

4

5

6

7

8

9

if it mak me ask it's goo

i used to go to a gym where
i'd see this guy who was always wearing
a T-shirt that said "free east timor."
in a way it made me angry, because
i assumed that he didn't even know
where east timor was, any more
than i do. what does it mean to have slogans
about important issues on a T-shirt? now i've
decided not to assume anything. he might
be a dedicated activist or he might be ignorant.

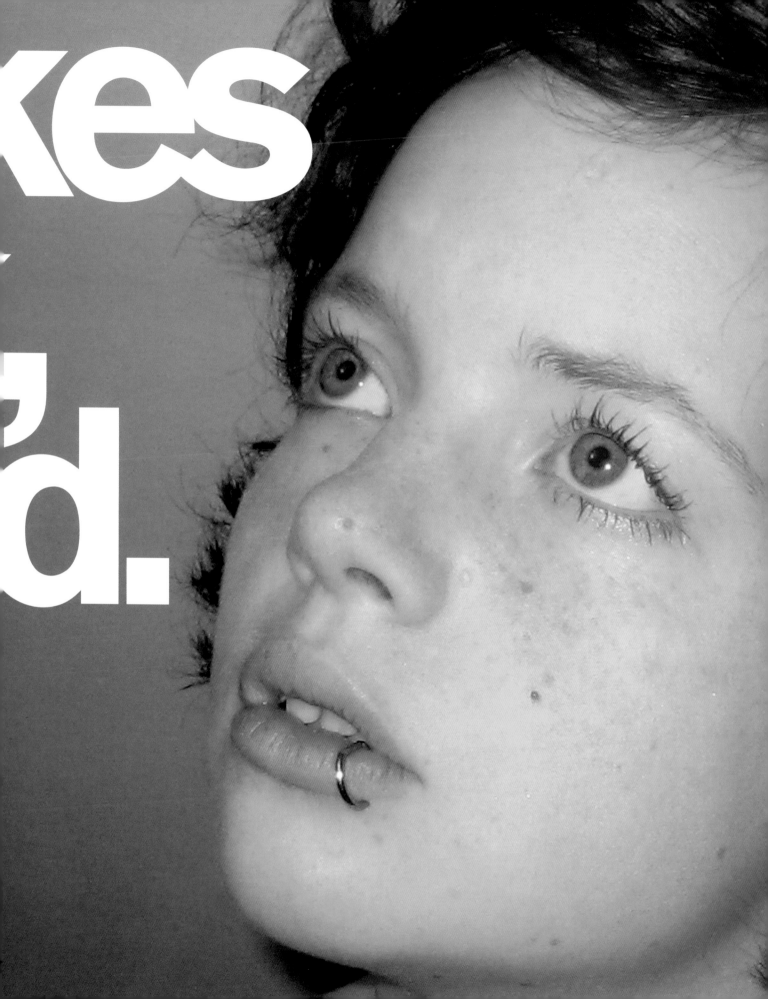

here are some
flirt cards
**cut them up,
give them out, and
see what develops.**

i like you.

i saw what you did.

i like you.

i saw what you did.

i like you.

i saw what you did.

i like you.

i saw what you did.

i like you.

my card.

wow.

my card.

wow.

my card.

wow.

my card.

wow.

my card.

wow.

yes.	turn around.
yes.	turn around.
yes.	turn around.
yes.	turn around.
yes.	turn around.

hi.

be still, my heart.

hi.

be still, my heart.

hi.

be still, my heart.

hi.

be still, my heart.

hi.

be still, my heart.

1. OUT

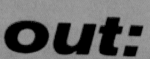

2. IN

out:

BAD
boys

in:
SAD
boys

fill these in as best you can. if you want to.

best friend ....

.... soft touch

scapegoat ....

fallback ....

.... ROLE MODEL

.... crush

PROTECTOR ....

IDOL ....

nemesis

....

doppelgänger ....

protégé

....

BÊTE NOIRE

....

HERO ....

best poem, ever.

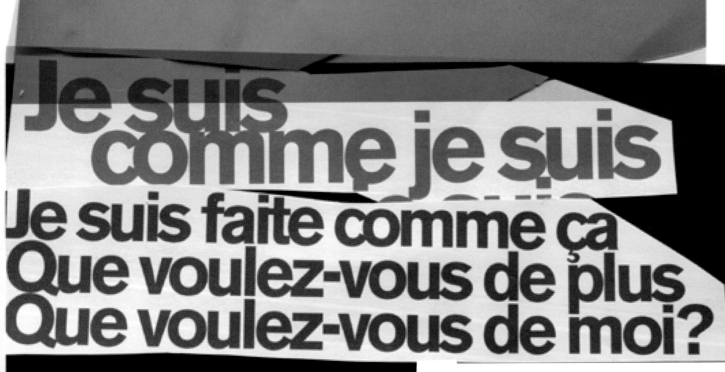

Je suis
comme je suis
Je suis faite comme ça
Que voulez-vous de plus
Que voulez-vous de moi?

Jacques Prévert

I am who I am
I am made
like this
What more
do you want?
What do you
want from
me?

by the way, when they say that you have to **LOVE*** *yourself* before someone else can love you,** it's just not true.

*LIKE is good enough.

** or before you can love
someone else, or whatever

I ♥ ME

so don't worry about it.

i can't tell
people to get involved.
i can't tell people
to be activists.
that would be
hypocritical.
i don't do anything.
i vote. i usually
recycle. but i don't
have children
and i don't have a car,
so maybe i am helping?
i plan to give back
when i get my own
stuff together but this
never seems to happen.
i worked in a soup
kitchen a few times.
but not many.
so hey kids, get involved!
be activists. do it for me.

OH, BOY.

A friend visited some distant relatives in Budapest. None of them spoke English, except for one cousin, István. They made a big family dinner in his honor. The meal was strangely pale: filet of sole, mashed potatoes, cauliflower, and, oddly, chocolate milk. You know how it is when you don't speak the language, you're just smiling like some kind of idiot, and thanking people. So he was grinning away, nodding yes to everything, and they kept pressing more and more food on him. He couldn't handle one more bite, but didn't want to say "No."

Instead, to show how full he was, he leaned back in his chair, stuck out his stomach, and patted it. And with a big smile on his face, he looked at everyone and said "OH BOY OH BOY OH BOY!" Suddenly, the entire table was struck dumb. In shock–just frozen. Horrified! Something bad had happened. So he asked István, "What? What's wrong? What did I do?" And István said, "Well, I don't know why, but you just leaned back in your chair and said,

'VAGINA VAGINA VAGINA!'"

By the way, I heard later from an actual Hungarian that "Oh Boy Oh Boy Oh Boy" sounds nothing like their word for vagina which is "Vagina."

...INES

You all make a big "responsible" point about telling us to accept ourselves the way we are and try not to be anorexic, and on the next page you're showing twelve-year-old girls wearing eight-thousand-dollar, size 0 outfits and carrying ten-thousand-dollar handbags. Also, you love articles that make us think we're dying. I call one of them *Young Hypochondriac Today*.

AND DON'T GET ME STARTED ON "SELF-HELP" BOOKS LIKE THIS!
YOU NEED THEM LIKE THE TURKEY NEEDS THE AX.

YOUR BREASTS: WHAT DO THEY **MEAN** ?

I'm not talking about *THE NEW YORKER*. or fun mags like *THE ECONOMIST*.

Everyone should read *THE NEW YORKER*.

REALLY EXTREME MAKEOVER:

25,185 DAYS

ARIES

aries are actors who live in hollywood. they bleach their teeth to an unnatural whiteness. even though they're pushy, egotistical, and loud, they're still bagging groceries at vons. their unspeakably bad screenplay will never be produced, which goes without saying. they're out running, but they can't run away from themselves. but you can run away from them. why don't you?

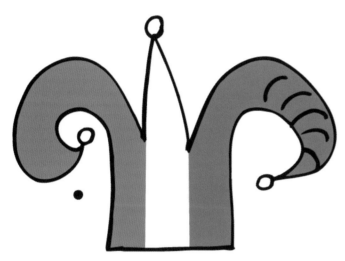

TAURUS

taurans are needy, self-conscious bureaucrats who always feel that they are being rushed. they have nothing to say, and don't hesitate to not say it.
if your banker is a taurus, you are lucky.
if your lover is a taurus, break out the heavy armor, lock all the windows, and put a chair against the door. you can play some mozart. it won't help. taureans wear colored contacts. they're not fooling anybody. one word: south beach diet.

GEMINI

they're shallow, unreliable, and never shut up. keep them away from broccoli, Krazy Glue, and scissors. if they're born in late may they should use a cream blusher. an ideal gemini career? court jester.

CANCER

according to Wikipedia, cancerians are changeable, moody, hypersensitive, touchy, patriotic, clingy and unable to let go, tenacious, devious, dominating, secretive, cold, overcritical, harsh, ruthless, suspicious, jealous, quick-tempered, violent, volatile, controlling, depressive, deceitful, lacking in stability, manipulative, aloof, dogmatic, eccentric, and overdramatic. they need a good undereye concealer. if that's not a reason to love Wikipedia, i don't know what is.

LEO

leos like to bask in the sunlight of adoration and are addicted to applause and sometimes peanut butter.
if they are not out prospecting for gold, you will find them in your bathroom going through your makeup bag. leos make their hair look bigger than it is. grrrrr. beware.

VIRGO

virgos smell like an old-fashioned health food store. the astrological symbol of virgo is said to represent the arms and torso of the virgin holding a sheaf of wheat. they think they are allergic to wheat. you can't even order pizza with a virgo, the sanctimonious prudes!

LIBRA

aren't you glad you're not a libra? me, too. on the other hand, they make great zookeepers and submarine operators. then again, they're violent. yet oddly adorable. they wear too much eyeliner. it's a toughie.

SAGITTARIUS

sagittarians are accident prone hypersensitive egomaniacs. they will develop severe tummy problems and/or be suspected of murder. they should pluck their eyebrows but don't. please don't play darts with a sag.

SCORPIO

on a good day a scorpio tends to be self-destructive, ruthless, overbearing, suspicious, jealous, possessive, moody, sadistic, insulting, secretive, intolerant, vindictive, and terribly insecure. don't get in the car.

also their nails are too pointy. ouch!

CAPRICORN

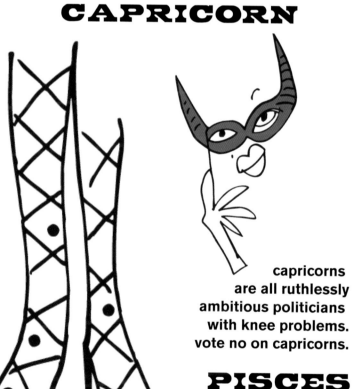

capricorns are all ruthlessly ambitious politicians with knee problems. vote no on capricorns.

AQUARIUS

fickle and perverted, all aquarians are alcoholics. because they are born under the constellation that was once ganymede, cupbearer of the gods, they use this as an excuse for heavy drinking. high maintenance highlights don't help.

PISCES

pisces are tiny little insignificant crybabies who always think they are being criticized. they're right.

FANTASTIC ILLUSTRATIONS BY **LENE DUE JENSEN**

i finally decided to get some clothes
that really fit me. so i go to saks . . . i hear
they've got a special department for size
14 and up. i think it's called "salon Z"
i go in the store and there's the . . . i don't
know what you call her . . . the info chick,
at this sort of podium thing.

and i say,

"where's your big fat
ugly girl department?"

and you know
what she

says?

sex!   death!

The trouble with love is that pets don't last long enough and people last too long.

HAMSTER

My parents were highly educated, liberal, sophisticated nincompoops. When I found out about death (hamsters?) I freaked out. What happens when you die? Is there a God? Is there a Heaven? They sat me down and carefully explained, "Well the Buddhists believe this, and the Christians believe that, and the Jews believe this, that, and the other thing, and the Muslims … " and so on. They wanted me to decide these things for myself. That's fine if you're seventeen. **but**

the point is
you cannot
explain

the finer points
of spirituality
to a
four year old!

They told me about sex when I was six. Clearly they were confused, or I was, because then I became a vegetarian. Much later I found out the way most people do. And now I think I've forgotten.

KICKED OUT OF YO9A

On the mat in front of each student was a small towel, a blanket, and a pink Kleenex. Everyone was deeply attuned to the instructor's soothing, hypnotic voice in the darkened room. "Hold one nostril and breathe in, then hold the other and breathe out."

I managed to keep a straight face. Right through the fish, the plow, downward facing dog, and warrior positions, up to and including the jumping frog. The teacher spoke softly, "Now everybody roll up your blankets." Obediently, we started rolling up the big heavy wool blankets. She gently corrected us, saying, "I said to roll your *towels*, please" pointing to the towels. I couldn't help myself, crying out for cosmic justice. "*But you said BLANKET!*" I started laughing uncontrollably. Couldn't stop. Suddenly, the teacher's voice rang out in the darkness; a voice with a not-so-new-age edge. "Perhaps there are some people here *WHO SHOULDN'T BE HERE RIGHT NOW.*" I removed my corporeal presence. I ran like the wind, and then I bought a Snickers. I never found out what the Kleenex was for. I was kicked out of Yoga class.

And I'm thinking,

this woman has just used up all of her superlatives! If it were me, I would wait until that piece of yellowtail jumped up, ran out onto Houston Street, hailed a cab to the airport, jumped on a flying fish roe, flew to the Middle East, created a lasting peace, came back, turned into Johnny Depp, stepped over the bodies of Jessica Alba, Scarlett Johansson, and Matt Damon, pulled the Hope Diamond out of his pocket, popped open a magnum of Chateau d'Yquem 1929, got down on one knee, and said, "LAURIE, WILL YOU BE MY BRIDE?"

Then, and only then, would I say, "You know what?

That yellowtail is AZING

far-out things to say instead of
AMAGING or AWESOME:

doozie
extravagant
fab
fantastic
gone
greatest
immense

superb
striking
bewildering
turn-on
breathtaking
startling
impressive
miraculous
spectacular
staggering

inconceivable
incredible
legendary
out-of-this-world

striking
stunning
wonderful
wondrous
outrageous
remarkable
spectacular
unbelievable

fabulous
far-out
superhuman
unreal
wonderful
hair-raising
thrilling
heart-stirring
jaw-dropping
impressive
magnificent
moving
overwhelming
spine-tingling
stunning

SUPER
STUPENDOUS

TOP DRAWER!

peachy

astonishing!

ASTOUNDING!

PRODIGIOUS!

more
just
plain
bizarre

Hello.
My name is_____
and I go to a
nut-free school.
I have been nut-free
at school
for seven years.

(Welcome!
We're all proud of you)

Anyway. People with
peanut butter allergies
should either die or,
you know, whatever.
Deal with it.
It's called survival
of the fittest,
and if you're going
to be defeated
by peanut butter,
you are not fit,
and Darwin says
you go to Hell.

In conclusion: gimme

my peanut butter.

STARTLING CONFESSION:

LTHOUGH i claim
to prize individuality, i use the
manufacturer's default settings for my
computer monitor and my cell phone screen
because i think this will make me more
normal. it makes me feel like I am
doing something right.

6 things

THAT BUG ME
(AND SOME RANDOM SILLINESS)

1 IN MOVIES
and on TV shows, people are constantly saying, "what are *you* doing here?"

and also, when the driver is talking to someone in the passenger or back seat and looking at them and it takes too long. this makes me nervous.

2 OTHER STUFF
when i type in microsoft word, i can't stop it from correcting me. i just don't like capital letters. in other respects i feel strongly about good grammar, spelling, and punctuation. my iPhone guesses wrong, too. i use unusual words and sometimes swedish. it turns them into usual ones. the horror! that, and being forced to look at advertising in the back of a cab or on the back of an airplane tray table, or anyplace where i can't shut it off and think my own thoughts.

3 time was, i used to be able to buy weirdly packaged shampoo and toothpaste and dish soap and things in foreign lands, with peculiar (and shocking) brand names. now everything's the same. this store (see bag, left) and so many others seem to be everyplace, so why travel? there's a web site called kioskkiosk.com that scours the world for things unavailable elsewhere. a dart game from finland! hot pink rubber gloves from mexico! old-school headphones from . . . someplace! on the other hand, the use of helvetica makes me feel clean and safe, although i use akzidenz grotesk. designers are afraid *not* to use helvetica, and i'm just as guilty as anyone.

4 the idiotic way corporations force humans to communicate. i once heard an airline pilot announce, "next time your travel plans include travel, we hope you'll think of us." my travel plans always include travel. aaargh!

apparently, as a child i was taken to the central park zoo, where i lay on the ground and tried to feed peanuts to the ants.

5 retouching. *nobody* glows like this. if they do, call the paramedics. my friend norman pointed out, "i never realized that *photoshop* made a filter called *basted turkey!*"

6 time gets shorter as you get older. never mind the sheepdog. i just wanted him in the book.

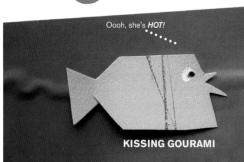

Oooh, she's *HOT!*

KISSING GOURAMI

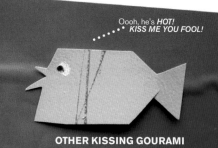

Oooh, he's *HOT!*
KISS ME YOU FOOL!

OTHER KISSING GOURAMI

guys shouldn't drink tea or eat soup. it makes them look like a

WUSS

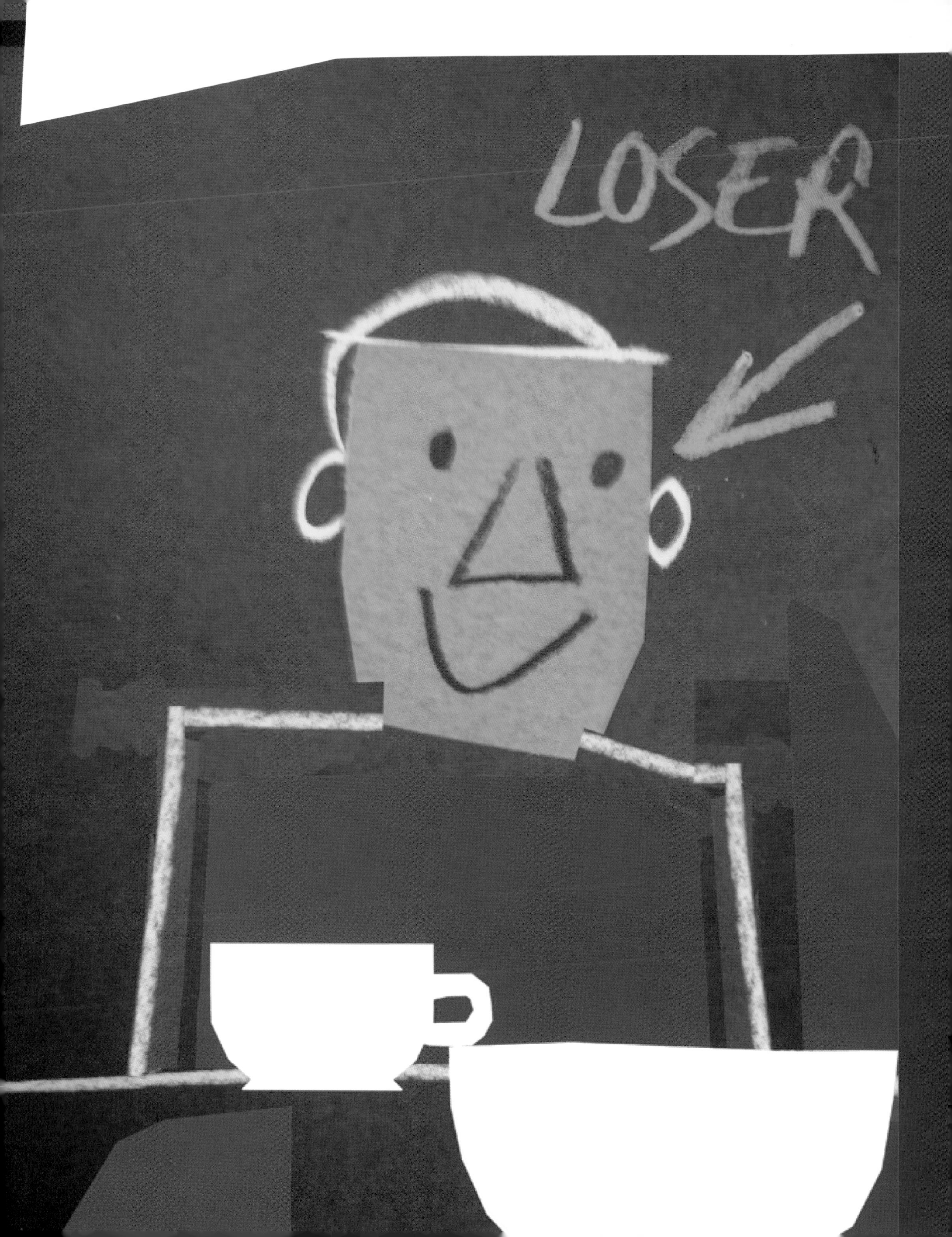
LOSER

BEAUTY, WHERE ARE YOU?

THERE WAS AN AD CAMPAIGN

on the internet that featured "real" girls. It was designed to promote self-esteem. I had a problem with it. They weren't ugly enough. They chose pretty girls who just weren't models, and said, "You're beautiful, too! Even though you're real!" But they didn't show really fat, ugly girls and say, "You're beautiful, too!" to *them*. In another ad, they showed how much retouching is done on all the beauty images we're bombarded with. It's good to be aware of these things, but I feel they were disingenuous, because in this "real" campaign they do the same thing, only more subtly. They are not exempt. Their real mission is to sell cosmetics. Keep that in mind.

Women are attracted to what they love, and men love what they're attracted to. Discuss

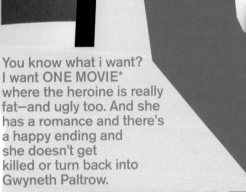

You know what i want? I want ONE MOVIE* where the heroine is really fat—and ugly too. And she has a romance and there's a happy ending and she doesn't get killed or turn back into Gwyneth Paltrow.

JUST ONE!

With all the open-mindedness about sexuality, this is one story you never, ever see.

IS THAT TOO MUCH TO

Remember
*REAL WOMEN
HAVE CURVES?
She's not fat
enough.

ASK?

EAUTY

is in the mind of the
beheld

you can go . . . until you go far.

–with apologies to (possibly) t. s. eliot
via gina roose

a girl i know was trying to remember a quote
to use on her yearbook page. i like her version better than the real thing.

they say,

"what goes around, comes around" but i don't know. i think it goes around, but then it just keeps going around.

things that bug me, part one:

just be yourself!

oh! there's another choice? then i'll be this lovely girl!

Just Because They Never Went Away Doesn't Mean We Can't Revive Them All Over Again. Because They're Due For A Comeback:

1. Ham (an appreciation)
2. The Night-light
3. Smocking
4. The Salt Lick
5. Richie Havens
6. Filet of Sole
7. Cheddar
8. Germany (former, West)
9. Naps

MY DAY:

shake for breakfast
iphone iphone iphone
texting
myspacemyspacemyspace
e-mail e-mail e-mail
time for ME
facebookfacebookfacebook
naptime
youtubeyoutubeyoutube
a quick shake
shake for lunch
and i'm done

super

and by the way, *why aren't all our teeth blindingly white by now?*

things that bug me, part deux:

this is a picture of a store window. it's hard to see here but the store window admonishes one to **"DO ONE THING A DAY THAT SCARES YOU"** um, excuse me, but last time i checked, it was not the job of the dreadful polo shirt purveyors to dispense life lessons, spout idiotic faux-zen platitudes, or tell me how to live my life. look! the mannequin has no head. perhaps it did one scary thing too many and was decapitated. so sell me some hideous chinos, shut up, and be gone.

things i like that maybe you'll like too:

books and authors
the pursuit of love
or love in a cold climate
by nancy mitford

up in the old hotel
by joseph mitchell

mapp and lucia
by e. f. benson

cold comfort farm
by stella gibbons

artists
saul steinberg
paul rand
stuart davis
william steig

movies
mon oncle
or play time
by jacques tati

sullivan's travels
by preston sturges

the producers
by mel brooks

best in show
by christopher guest

nights of cabiria
or juliet of the spirits
directed by federico fellini

north by northwest
or vertigo
directed by alfred hitchcock

i think people say "i love you" too much. like every time they hang up the phone!

there are two versions of me. there is the TEMPORARY me. she's the one you see every day: fat, ugly, and wearing boring, unfashionable black clothes. then there's the REAL me! the REAL me is glamorous, thin, beautiful, and wears the hippest clothes. but for right now, you will have to look at the TEMPORARY me, because i am not ready to be the REAL me. i must get thin first so i can fit into those clothes. i know exactly which designers i'll wear. while i'm waiting, i know that the real chic, fabulous me is inside, so i don't feel bad about my TEMPORARY image. what people see now is not the REAL me. this has been going on for my whole life, just wait till you see the beautiful REAL ME. pretty soon!

canary

add chaos to your order
or, HOW TO MAKE MISTAKES ON PURPOSE

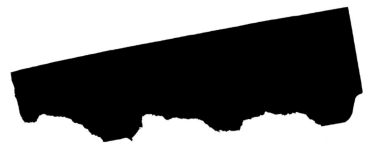

I teach a workshop
called "**How to Make Mistakes
on Purpose.**" I can't really
describe it (top secret) but
it has something to do with the
idea that if you really focus
on what you're doing and try
super hard to succeed at
whatever it is, it will probably
turn out bad (for me, anyhow).
So in my workshops we're bad on
purpose. There's a power in wrong
things. They're full of surprises!

For example, for my picture book,
*And to Name but Just a Few:
Red, Yellow, Green, Blue,* I had to
draw a canary. So like every other person
on earth, I went to Google images and
out popped ten thousand canaries.
I don't use them. Instead I
find some random ripped paper
I have lying around, take one that looks
nothing like a canary (see which one?),
color it yellow (in computer), stick
an eyeball and legs and a beak on it,
put the word "canary" in
500 point type next to it, and
you better believe it's
a bleeping canary.
Computers (we all use them)
can't make mistakes,
so how can you be surprised?
It's not just about artwork,
it applies to everything.
Also, I have a fear of the blank page.
I feel like I can't draw, but if I
have something (anything)
to start with, like these random
shapes, I can. Much of this book was
done this way. It's full of misyakes!

AKNOWLEDGMENTS
THANK
YOU

extra extra thanks to:

GINA ROOSE
GUNNEL SAHLIN
DOVANNA PAGOWSKI
CATHY LINSK
LENE DUE JENSEN
MARIA LUNDBERG
GUS PETERSEN
NICOLE GASTONGUAY

olive panter
helene silverman
anna giouroukou
karin giouroukou
norman hathaway
wilma hathaway
stefan rosén
tove due rosén
tove ramhöj larsson
ed stern
pär johansson
jenny, amanda
and elias werne
emma roose
david ray
malcolm ray
justina ray
michele collins
julia kylén-collins
josephine kylén-collins
johan kyléns
julian biber
carin goldberg
dorothée lalanne
jo viemeister
beata alfredsson grahn
jessika berglund
lo brandt

per & norea petersson
filip pagowski
kamila pagowski
erin an
michelizabet sainvill
jennifer unter
paula kelly
geneva bielenberg
jane nisselson
cyrus highsmith
annika petersen
michael bartalos
philippe lardy
augusta lardy
georgia read
tschabalala self
solveig fernlund
arvid logan
bibbi forsman
cornelia forsman
amanda alwan
jack, natalia, lisi
and delaney becker

nate turner
jonathan blum
dr. joseph linsk
karin hedberg
vera yuan
hjalti karlsson
dagur
ian dury
jacques prevert
jenny, amanda,
and elias werne
steve stein
vida behar
zoe kintisch rodruiguez

every attempt has
been made
to gain permissions and
give proper credit
to everyone involved
in this book.
if cases exist
where this has
not been accomplished,
it's not for lack of trying,
and we offer our
most sincere apologies.

de ungas akademi

benjamin palmblad
cecila nagny
nader pahlevani
justine bonnaya
jessica sander
olivia whitehouse
rebecka wendelsten
sofia atenas
rebecca n levén

anna rådvik
sofia åhrman

sigga sigurdjonsdottir
and the wonderful students from

the iceland
academy of art

not the author   the author

and to
jill davis,
in the cut-throat world of children's book publishing, the most brilliant, charming and generous of editors, the largest "thank you" of all!

Laurie Rosenwald has the patience of a saint, the hands of a surgeon, and a heart you could pour on a waffle. And, except for the shoplifting, she has a lot of personal integrity. She has never been a teenager. She has never had a teenager of her own and has no idea what they want. The product of a progressive education, she types four words a minute.

She is a regular subscriber to *Miniature Donkey Magazine* and can speak Swedish like a native New Yorker. She explains: "If you're from Topeka, you can go to Kansas City. If you're from Kansas City, you can go to Chicago. If you're from Chicago, you can go to New York. But if you're from Manhattan, where can you go?" Apparently, by the time she was 35 she had to go to Sweden just to calm down. She spends time in Gothenburg, but mostly, she lives in New York.

Born to beatniks, and an accomplished painter since the tender age of two, she teaches an incredibly popular workshop called "How to Make Mistakes on Purpose." It has been taught from Stockholm to Starbucks, RISD to Reykjavik. Visit www.rosenworld.com, where you will find more information, but not much. Workshop participants are sworn to secrecy.

Her illustrations have appeared in *The New Yorker*, *The New York Times*, and many other fine publications. She does quite a bit of advertising work in Europe because they don't understand her here. Her *New York Notebook* is a NYC guidebook, sketchbook and journal all mushed up together. Her picture book, *And To Name but Just a Few: Red, Yellow, Green, Blue* was named a Scholastic Parent & Child Best Book of 2007. She portrayed the arguably pivotal role of "Woman" on the season five opener of "The Sopranos," a role she was born to play. She has been a professor in both the Graphic Design and Illustration departments (what's the diff?) at both the Parsons School of Design and The School of Visual Arts. Rosenwald is principal of the design studio called rosenworld. Actually there is no studio, she usually works alone, and rosenworld doesn't exist. In spite of this, www.rosenworld.com was launched to great fanfare in 1995. No one knows where the money goes.

www.rosenworld.com
There she will entertain visitors.
Read the stories.

mary had a little lamb. it's fleece was white as snow. and everywhere that mary went, the lamb made a terrible scene.